MOVIE · POSTER · BOOK

Heart Throbs

TIM PULLEINE

OCTOPUS BOOKS

Acknowledgements

The publishers wish to thank the following for supplying the photographs in this book:

Aquarius Film Agency 6 right, 8 centre and right, 12 left, 22 left and right, 24 right, 25, 26 right, 28 right, 36 centre and left, 42 centre, 44 left, 46 centre; Camera Press (Terry O'Neill) 6 left, 32 right, 34 centre and right, 40 left, 48 left; Colorific Photo Library (Annie Leibovitz) 39; John Hillelson Agency Ltd (Dennis Stock) 17, 18 right; Kobal Collection 6 centre, 7, 8 left, 9, 10 centre and right, 14 centre, 15, 16 left and centre, 18 centre, 19, 20, 21, 22 centre, 23, 24 left and centre, 26 left and centre, 27, 28 left and centre, 29, 30 left and centre, 32 left and centre, 33, 34 left, 35, 36 left, 38, 40 centre, 41, 42 right, 45, 46 right, 47, 48 centre and right; National Film Archive, London 5, 43; The Photo Source 10 left, 12 right, 44 centre, 46 left; Rex Features 12 centre, 13, 14 left and right, 18 left, 42 left, 44 right; Transworld Feature Syndicate (UK) Ltd (Henry Grossman) 11, (Steve Schapiro) 31.

First published in 1985 by Octopus Books Limited
59 Grosvenor Street London W1

© 1985 Octopus Books Limited

ISBN 0 7064 2370 4

First impression

Printed in Hong Kong

·CONTENTS·

·INTRODUCTION·

Heart throbs…the term is, perhaps, rather old-fashioned, but the concept has never dated. All the men featured in the ensuing pages have one thing in common – that indefinable quality called sex appeal. If one attempted a definition, then one could only say what it is *not*. It has little to do with the merits or otherwise of the acting ability of the stars, nor necessarily with conventional good looks.

Although men are not as subject to changes in modes of dress as women are, nonetheless fashions in male love objects have varied greatly over the years. Humphrey Bogart once said, 'I came out here with one suit and everybody said I looked like a bum. Twenty years later, Marlon Brando comes out with only a sweat shirt and the town drools over him. That shows how much Hollywood has progressed'. Yet, Bogart himself had broken the mold by becoming a romantic lead despite his type-cast gangster face. 'How can a man so ugly be so handsome?' asks Marta Toren of Bogart in *Sirocco*. His lived-in face has thrilled as much as Clark Gable's protruding ears and con-man moustache, Elvis Presley's voluptuous lips or Paul Newman's steely blue eyes. Today, Rudolph Valentino's slicked down hair and made-up hypnotic brown eyes may seem risible to some, but visitors still flock every year to his phallic memorial in Hollywood.

Male vamp Valentino, at a time when athletic all-American boys like Douglas Fairbanks dominated the screen, injected a dose of Latin passion into pictures. Of course, his early death, like that of James Dean's three decades later, enhanced his status as a legend, freezing him forever in one moment of time. But whether they are legends, romantic heroes or role models, male stars have often had a bigger pull at the box-office than their female counterparts. Their appeal is to men almost as much as to women – icons for men to envy or emulate, and for women to dream about.

It is in their rapport with women on screen and, by proxy, with those in the audience, that heart throbs can best be assessed. They can be divided into three broad categories: Male Chauvinists, Gentlemen, and Rebels. The last group, which includes men like Marlon Brando, James Dean, Clint Eastwood and Steve McQueen, seem to exist apart from the women who might fetter their independence. Male Chauvinists, such as Clark Gable, Errol Flynn, Burt Reynolds and Sean Connery (as James Bond) are sexual beings bent on conquest. The Gentlemen, however, like Cary Grant, Gary Cooper, Robert Redford and Christopher Reeve, are dream dates, subjecting women to no pressures, offering a civilized, romantic relationship with sexual undertones. Unlike the way men have viewed female sex symbols, women have traditionally judged men on what they do and how they do it, rather than on how much body they reveal. But whatever the gender or tastes of moviegoers, they would all admit that most of the stars in this book make life more glamorous and the heart beat quicker.

· WARREN BEATTY ·

· WARREN BEATTY ·

Born **Richmond, Virginia, 30 March 1937**

'Sensual around the lips and pensive around the brow' was how the critic Kenneth Tynan described him after his 1959 Broadway debut in *A Loss Of Roses*. In terms of physical appearance, the young Beatty – with his even, slightly fleshy features and luxuriant dark hair – somewhat resembled the male pin-ups of a decade before, such as Rock Hudson or Tony Curtis. At the same time, though, he belonged to a somewhat different acting tradition: both *A Loss Of Roses* and the film *Splendor In The Grass* (1961) which marked his first screen appearance were of the then fashionable school of Freudian melodrama (*Splendor* was made by Elia Kazan, who had previously worked with both Brando and Dean.)

Beatty could claim readily that acting ran in his family: he is the younger brother of Shirley MacLaine, and their mother was a drama coach. Although in his early years as a movie actor Beatty sometimes played conventional romantic leads (as in *Promise Her Anything*, 1966), there was clear evidence that he wanted to do more. In fact, his second film role, in the Tennessee Williams adaptation, *The Roman Spring of Mrs Stone* (1962), found him playing a professional gigolo, a part in which his good looks were used to devastating effect on Vivien Leigh. In *Mickey One* (1965) Beatty ventured bravely into the murky depths of paranoid fantasy, but it was his subsequent collaboration with the same director, Arthur Penn, which marked a key turning point. This time Beatty was producer as well as star and the result was *Bonnie And Clyde*

(1967), one of the most admired and influential American movies for many a year. Nobody could say that Beatty's playing of bank robber Clyde Barrow, club-footed and impotent, yielded anything to conventional charm, but he could not disguise his powerful charisma. The movie achieved near-instant cult status – and at 30, Warren Beatty was very much a force to reckon with in the film industry.

The star's adventurousness continued to assert itself. He wrote, produced and starred in the mordant comedy *Shampoo* (1975), playing a role which seemed to mock his own off-screen status in the gossip columns as a ladies' man: one of his co-stars was Julie Christie, with whom his name was at one time romantically linked. *Heaven Can Wait* (1979) found him trying his hand at direction, though the film proved a rather ordinary comedy. Next, though, he embarked on directing a veritable epic, *Reds* (1982), himself playing John Reed, the American journalist who famously covered the Russian revolution of 1917. The film – in which his leading lady was Diane Keaton, another actress with whom he was for some time associated in private life – was made on a grand scale, and ambitiously incorporated testimony from survivors of the period it described, though it eventually met with a rather mixed critical reception.

Beatty hardly looks to be nearing 50; and it seems a fair bet that as he moves further into middle age, he will continue to have a few tricks up his attractive sleeve.

· HUMPHREY BOGART ·

· H U M P H R E Y   B O G A R T ·

Born **New York City, 23 January 1899** Died **14 January 1957**

Given the legend of 'Bogey' that has proliferated since his death, it can come as something of a surprise to discover that Humphrey Bogart began his acting career as an 'Anyone for tennis?' juvenile lead, if not, by all accounts, a very accomplished one. He was in fact the scion of a well-to-do Manhattan family – his father was a surgeon – though he was an early non-conformist to the extent of being expelled from the fashionable school which was to have been his springboard to a medical career.

After World War I service in the navy – a naval accident caused the lip injury that gave him his distinctive lisp and incipient snarl – he prevailed on a family friend to give him work in the theatre. Bogart first appeared in films in 1930, though not to any great effect. His break came when Leslie Howard cast him as the gangster Duke Mantee in the play *The Petrified Forest* – Bogart bore a more than passing resemblance to the then notorious Mid-West bank robber John Dillinger – and Howard later insisted that he should repeat the role in the 1936 movie version. Even so, Bogart remained a stock 'heavy' at Warners until, by lucky accident, George Raft chose to refuse the lead in *High Sierra* (1941) because he didn't want to die at the end. The part of a doomed mobster finding a romantic focus in life in the course of his last job fell to Bogart, and brought out in him a striking combination of the hard-bitten and soft-centred which was to prove so attractive to his numerous fans. The same year, his playing of the private

eye in *The Maltese Falcon* clinched his reputation.

The 1940s were the heyday of the smoky, sensual melodramas now known as *film noir*, and in this atmosphere Bogart's star kept rising – as the world-weary bar-owner of *Casablanca* (1943), and as Raymond Chandler's Philip Marlowe in *The Big Sleep* (1946), co-starring in the latter with his fourth and last wife, the considerably younger and very alluring Lauren Bacall. (His three previous marriages, all to actresses, had been brief and allegedly tempestuous.)

Bogart was comparatively short in stature and his face was accurately enough described by Howard Hawks, director of *The Big Sleep*, as 'homely'. But he could uncannily project a laconic exterior which seemed to mask an underlying fund of concern; and he could, as Chandler put it, 'be tough without a gun'. To an extent the star seems, in his later years, to have believed in his own publicity image, and to have essayed in public life the role of what the actress Louise Brooks unkindly called 'a coarse and drunken bully'.

But on several occasions during the latter part of his career – as the gin-sozzled Charlie Allnut in *The African Queen* (1952) or the paranoid Captain Queeg in *The Caine Mutiny* (1954) – he achieved character performances of real originality. And if the legend has sometimes been writ too large, and maybe caricatured in the process, the fact that it remains potent almost 30 years after his death testifies to something more than the power of the publicist.

· MARLON BRANDO ·

·MARLON BRANDO·

Born Omaha, Nebraska, 3 April 1924

To say that Marlon Brando looms large in the consciousness of any movie devotee might now, in the light of the ungainly, muffle-voiced figure of films like *Superman* (1978) and *Apocalypse Now* (1980), seem like a lame pun. Yet no post-war actor has left so unmistakably personal an imprint on the cinema. Of course, he has frequently been lampooned – in the early days of his fame, impersonations of a 'mumble and scratch' style of acting were a staple for comedians – but the performances themselves prove, when revisited, to be triumphantly able to withstand any such parody.

There have essentially been three Brandos, but first and foremost there was the actor who, at the age of only 23, took Broadway by storm as Stanley Kowalski in *A Streetcar Named Desire*, a performance he was to recreate for the film version of four years later. It is amazingly detailed playing and intensely physical: Kowalski is an animalistic character and Brando brought an animal power to the role.

Even in repose, the young Brando's slightly Oriental features had a brooding quality, a sense of unease and perhaps of threat. And in his mode of life, he chose to reject the then conventional trappings of stardom, wearing ripped tee-shirts, riding a motor-bike, and earning the epithet of 'slob'. (Brando was the son of a businessman father and a stage-struck mother; one of his elder sisters, Jocelyn, had preceded him on to the stage.) The image of the outsider, the rebel, persisted in the once notorious bike-gang movie *The Wild One* (1953) and,

more significantly, in Elia Kazan's classic, *On The Waterfront* (1954). But the actor, already a huge star, was clearly unwilling to be circumscribed by it: he played in Shakespeare (*Julius Caesar*, 1953), a musical (*Guys And Dolls*, 1955), even impersonated a Japanese (*Teahouse Of The August Moon*, 1957). Later, he was his own director for *One-Eyed Jacks* (1961), an extraordinary Western dominated by his sultry presence and his capacity for pain.

But the 1960s saw Brando's star decline. In private life he was involved in stormy relationships, failed marriages, and litigation; on the screen (he has not returned to the stage) the projects he selected were all too often misconceived, though there were exceptions, films like *Reflections In A Golden Eye* (1967), co-starring with Elizabeth Taylor, where the old magic shone through the middle-aged spread. Then in the early 70s came a double revelation. On the one hand, the all-but-unrecognisable Mafia patriarch of *The Godfather* (1971), character drawing in the fullest sense; on the other, the daringly raw exposure of nerves and emotions in the notorious *Last Tango In Paris* (1972), a performance as magnetic and as sensual as his Kowalski of 20 years before, and as sexually attractive to his army of fans of both sexes.

Since then, Brando seems increasingly to have receded into his own outsize shell. Undoubtedly he is a difficult figure, both personally and professionally. But he was, and is, a true original, and there aren't too many of them about.

· RICHARD BURTON ·

· RICHARD BURTON ·

Real Name **Richard Jenkins**
Born **Pontrhydfen, South Wales, 10 November 1925** Died **5 August 1984**

Quite probably Richard Burton is doomed to go down in popular history as the high-spending consort of Elizabeth Taylor and the expansive boyo from the Welsh Valleys who drank his way to hardy annual status in the gossip columns. There can be no denying that in some respects the flamboyant Burton was a latterday John Barrymore, frittering away his talent and becoming a clown prince of the media – but that was far from the whole story.

Burton took his professional name from the schoolmaster who helped him to an Oxford scholarship, and he once told an interviewer that perhaps really he should have been a professor of literature. The remark gives some indication of how seriously he felt about the classics; and indeed in 1966 he enlisted the aid of none other than Professor Nevil Coghill in making a film of *Dr Faustus*.

Yet in practice Burton seemed made for acting. He first won acclaim on the stage for *The Lady's Not For Burning* in 1949, and his playing in *Hamlet* and *Henry IV* at the Old Vic in the early 1950s elicited extraordinary praise: he was seen as having at least the potential of a new Olivier. Of not especially impressive stature, Burton possessed litheness and an intense physical magnetism – a face and eyes that can only be called beautiful and, above all, a wonderful vocal range. His looks made him a natural for films – he had appeared in several British pictures before making his Hollywood debut in *My Cousin Rachel* (1952), opposite Olivia de Havilland – and he easily adapted to screen acting. The pity is that he was generally restricted to portentous costume movies like *The Robe* (1953) and *Alexander The Great* (1955) – he undeniably looked well in an abbreviated toga – or to nonsense like *The Rains Of Ranchipur* (1955), in which, several years before Peter Sellers patented the model, he essayed the role of an Indian doctor. Yet back in Britain for *Look Back In Anger* (1959), he provided, even though he was a little old for the 'angry young man', Jimmy Porter, a performance blazing with anguished feeling: to see it again now is to be forcefully reminded of what Burton might have been.

Not long afterwards he was cast as Mark Antony in the epic *Cleopatra* (1963). Making the film in Rome, he fell in love with his co-star Elizabeth Taylor, and the consequences are scarcely unknown: scandal, divorce, a marriage to Taylor distinguished by orgies of conspicuous consumption, a succession of films together at phenomenal salaries. The couple divorced in 1973, remarried in 1975, divorced again the next year. For Burton during the 1970s there were severe bouts of alcoholism which doubtless contributed to his premature death, and parts in a polyglot string of frequently dreadful movies. But there were exceptions, notably the psychiatrist in *Equus* (1977). And in his last, posthumously released, film, *1984*, his playing of the interrogator was a chillingly pared-down portrait of ideological mania. Alas, though, fate denied him the chance to make it a new professional beginning.

· SEAN CONNERY ·

· SEAN CONNERY ·

Real name **Thomas Connery**
Born **Edinburgh, 25 August 1930**

For a generation of filmgoers, Sean Connery *was* James Bond, 007, licensed to kill. This was not quite an overnight sensation – it was the second Bond film, *From Russia With Love* (1983), more than the first, *Dr No* (1962), which really got the Bondwagon rolling – but once the label stuck, it stuck tight. Throughout the 1960s, as the budgets soared and the effects became increasingly fantastic, the Bond movies grew into an institution, with Connery enshrined, lethal and mocking, at their profitable centre. Not such a soft centre, either. As *Time Magazine* so characteristically phrased it, Connery 'moves with a tensile grace that excitingly suggests the violence that is bottled in Bond'.

Connery had been virtually unknown when *Dr No* came out. After a working-class Scots upbringing, he joined the Navy, becoming a service boxing champion, and subsequently worked at labouring jobs. But he also took up body-building, and this led him to assignments as a male model: the combination perhaps points forward to the mixture of physique and gracefulness which marked his Bond. Later, Connery turned to acting, beginning a little improbably with a spell in the chorus of the London production of *South Pacific*. Some minor film roles followed, and a good deal of TV: interestingly, in a TV production of *Dark Victory* he played the role which had been Humphrey Bogart's in the movie version.

His enlistment as 007 was on pragmatic grounds: the producers couldn't afford a star name. As it turned out, Connery rapidly became one, with bargaining power to match. He was, moreover, wise enough to distance himself from Bond in other films: in *Marnie* (1964), Hitchcock fully exposed the saturnine sexuality which the Bond films cushioned in facetiousness and gadgetry. He even chanced his arm playing a manic poet in *A Fine Madness* (1966) and managed to look an authentic cowboy hero, opposite Bardot, in the European Western, *Shalako* (1968).

The actor has proved an astute businessman as well as a sometimes adventurous artist. After supposedly abandoning Bond, he was able to demand phenomenal terms for a comeback in *Diamonds Are Forever* in 1971. During the ensuing decade, he gravitated toward character roles, unabashed on several occasions at shedding his toupee and revealing himself to be nearly bald. His capacity gently to send himself up was displayed by his Arab chieftain in *The Wind And The Lion* (1975), as was his continuing grace and agility. He is in fact a devoted golfer, and can certainly afford to play on the best courses.

Connery, who was married during the 1960s to actress Diane Cilento, now lives with his second wife in Spain and Switzerland, and is apparently on the best of terms with his Bond successor, Roger Moore. He returned again (though surely finally) to 007 in his own production of *Never Say Never Again* in 1983: it was a good-natured enterprise but somehow the old flame had burned a bit low.

· GARY COOPER ·

· GARY COOPER ·

Real name **Frank Cooper**
Born **Helena, Montana, 7 May 1901** Died **13 May 1961**

The dyed-in-the-wool stereotype conjured by the mention of Gary Cooper is of a stetson-hatted figure whose vocabulary seldom extended beyond 'Yup' and 'Nope', but it does him considerably less than justice. True, Cooper (the son of a judge) was a Westerner in real life – although part of his boyhood was spent in England – as well as in several memorable movies like *The Plainsman* (1937), in which he played Wild Bill Hickock and, most famously of all, *High Noon* (1952). But both on and off the screen there were sundry other sides to him.

Strangely enough, Cooper's ambition as a young man was to be a cartoonist, but once in California he took on odd jobs, which included working as an extra in cowboy pictures. He graduated to featured roles as a heavy in two-reel Westerns, then was cast in a major production, *The Winning Of Barbara Worth* (1926). A small part as a tough flying instructor in the aviation epic *Wings* (1927) consolidated his new-found position and he acceded to the ranks of Hollywood's leading men, where he would remain for over three decades.

Very tall and lean, with a laconically etched profile, Coop (as he was known) did not have any formal training as an actor, but he was one of those comparatively rare performers whom the camera instantly loves. He was, in short, a screen natural, though he was also, in the words of Henry Hathaway who directed him in several movies, 'the most under-rated actor I've ever worked with'. Between 1930 and 1937, he did not actually make a single Western, but played with skill in romances, comedies, and as the archetypal small-town hero in Frank Capra's *Mr Deeds Goes To Town* (1936). Romance was, moreover, reputed to be Cooper's forte in private life. In his early days of stardom, his name was linked with such glamorous ladies as Clara Bow and Lupe Velez; as Budd Schulberg engagingly put it, 'for all his quiet speech and diffident ways, Coop might have been the Babe Ruth of the Hollywood boudoir league'. Before too long, however, he settled into matrimony with the former socialite Veronica Balfe, even though some years later this was temporarily ruffled by his much publicised affair with Patricia Neal, his co-star in *The Fountainhead* (1949).

Cooper's screen career dipped somewhat in the post-war years, but recovered with *High Noon*, for which he won his second Oscar (the first was for *Sergeant York*, 1941). He was visibly ageing, but could still essay both adventure movies (*Vera Cruz*, 1954) and a romantic comedy (*Love In The Afternoon*, 1957) with the old style intact, though it is a pity that his last film, *The Naked Edge* (1961), should have been so indifferent. He was a professional for whom nobody seemed to have a bad word – a real star and a real gentleman.

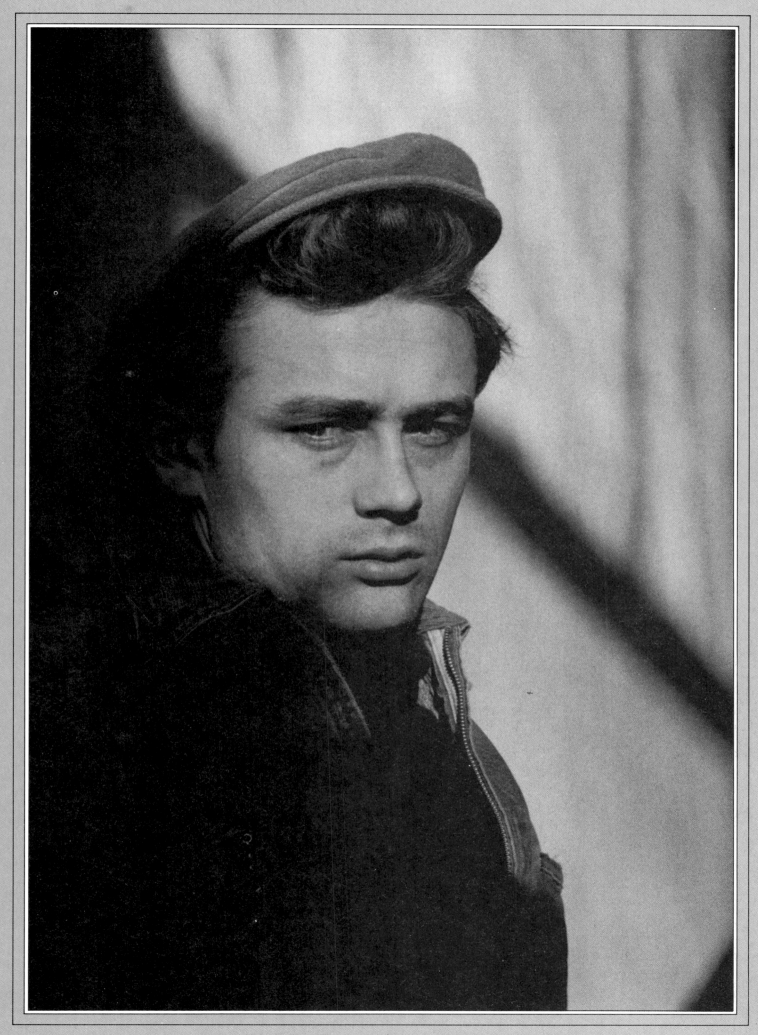

· JAMES DEAN ·

· JAMES DEAN ·

Born **Marion, Indiana, 8 February 1931** Died **30 September 1955**

It is a unique phenomenon. James Dean died in a car smash at the age of 24, after starring in only three films: a year before his death he had been an unknown. He had been in the public eye for an infinitely shorter period than Rudolph Valentino, the world's most famous heart-throb and the obvious comparison; yet three decades later, Dean's reputation as one of the great icons of the movies is unchallenged. Of course, it was partly the fact that he died in the bloom of youth that explains his mystique: he remains forever young, and his death insured us against any possibility of our disillusionment with him.

Dean belonged to his time – to the 1950s, the era in which youth culture and its concomitant of fashionable nonconformity began to burgeon under the emblems of rock'n'roll music and high-powered motorbikes. In some respects, Dean was the natural successor to Marlon Brando, whom he greatly admired. Like Brando, he studied at the Actors' Studio, home of the 'Method' and, again like Brando, his career took off under the tutelage of Elia Kazan, director of *East Of Eden* (1954), the film in which Dean, co-starred with Julie Harris, burst forth as a fully fledged star presence, ablaze with a mingled vulnerability and egotistic assertion.

Vulnerability was perhaps built into Dean's upbringing. His mother died when he was eight and he was brought up by an aunt and uncle. It would no doubt be simplistic to suggest that he was searching for a mother substitute in the succession of unhappy romances that littered his short path through life. But there was undoubtedly something of the little boy lost about him as an object of desire and identification.

Although *East Of Eden* was a period film, set during World War I, Dean struck a reverberatingly contemporary nerve, and his second and most celebrated film, *Rebel Without A Cause* (1955), was contemporary to the core. Intense almost to the point of expresssionism in its evocation of a secret world of teenage rivalry, it provided a perfect showcase for its star's capacity to project a mixture of outgoing tenderness, and incoming pain and frustration. Yet Dean was 23 and playing a character of presumably about 17: he was in a sense on borrowed time so far as his popular identity was concerned.

However, in his third and final film, *Giant* (1956), the actor was called upon to extend his range. In the early scenes, he is still the youthful loner, but the lengthy timespan converts him eventually into a dissipated, middle-aged oil tycoon, and his capacity to suggest the frailty of the prematurely aged man is startling. One senses here that Dean had an acting potential at least the equal of Brando's.

Alas, we shall never know. Just after completing his work in *Giant*, he crashed the Porsche he so loved to drive at high speed. But if James Dean's death robbed us of a potentially major actor, it froze him in a posture of romantic yearning which has not since been surpassed.

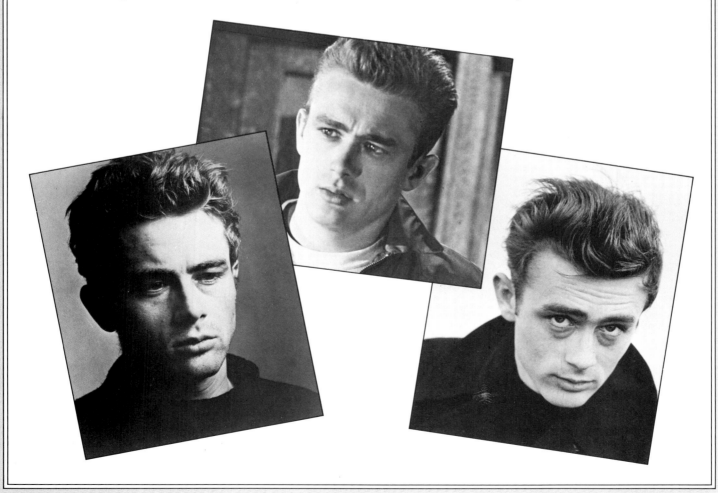

· CLINT EASTWOOD ·

· CLINT EASTWOOD ·

Born **San Francisco, 31 May 1930**

A chewed cheroot, a ragged poncho, several days' growth of stubble: these were the unusual, not to say unsavoury, emblems of Clint Eastwood's rise to super-stardom as the *Man With No Name* in the trio of 'spaghetti Westerns' inaugurated by *A Fistful Of Dollars* (1964). These potboiling Italian movies became an international cult and made Eastwood into a definitive modern anti-hero.

On his home ground, Eastwood's earlier image, insofar as he could be said to have one, had been conventionally clean cut. He had drifted into acting after an itinerant childhood and a spell as an air force swimming instructor, and had made a modest reputation in a TV Western series, *Rawhide*. His movie appearances, though, had been limited to some small supporting roles, in one of which he was apparently required to don spectacles so as not to detract from the allure of the softer, prettier Rock Hudson.

But on the strength of the *Dollar* trilogy, he returned to the US with not just a new persona but a bankable name – and his instincts were accurate enough for him to make himself a powerful force in the film industry, not only as an actor but as a producer and director too.

Eastwood's first solid American hit was the cop thriller *Dirty Harry*, made in 1971. The film cleaned up its star's physical appearance while reiterating his lean, macho sexuality, and went on to clean up at the box-office. But in it Eastwood's

personality remained challengingly ambiguous. At any rate, the film was the subject of some simple-minded attacks for its supposed endorsement of vigilante justice. Eastwood was turned 40 when *Dirty Harry* came out. But like some of his predecessors – Cary Grant is a prime case in point – he seems to gain in presence and looks as he grows older. He is unmistakably a movie star in the old sense, perhaps the last in that particular line – someone whose very appearance in a film guarantees an audience.

In the early 70s however, he was far from ready to coast along on his own success. The same year as *Dirty Harry*, Eastwood turned director with *Play Misty For Me*, unexpectedly casting himself as a womanising disc jockey who almost winds up a corpse. A little later (1976) came *The Outlaw Josey Wales*, a revenge Western of sweep and scope which posited Clint as the natural heir to John Wayne (and in which he co-starred with Sondra Locke, 17 years his junior, who became his companion in private life).

Since then, some of his more recent ventures have been into redneck farce, calculatedly offbeat whimsy like *Honky-tonk Man* (1982), an indication, perhaps, that Eastwood, now attractively but very visibly advancing into his 50s, is grasping rather strenuously at novelty. However, *Escape From Alcatraz* (1979) showed his wry, understated machismo still at full throttle. We must hope for the best …

· ERROL FLYNN ·

· ERROL FLYNN ·

Born **Hobart, Tasmania, 20 June 1909** Died **14 October 1959**

The legacy that Errol Flynn bequeathed to popular culture is a strangely divided one. One the one hand there is the apogee of the swashbuckler, an athletic *Boy's Own* embodiment of romantic heroism, especially as Robin Hood in the 1939 film. On the other, there is the dissolute athlete of a different kind, commemorated in the catchphrase 'In like Flynn', whose supposed attributes provided for years a staple topic of bar-room, and doubtless powder-room, speculation.

Born to a well-to-do Australian family, Flynn nonetheless led a scapegrace early life in such pursuits as searching for gold in New Guinea. His looks caused him to be selected, when he was 24, to play Fletcher Christian in a low-budget Australian movie, *In The Wake Of The Bounty*. Bitten by the acting bug, he sailed for England and within a couple of years had progressed from a Northampton repertory theatre company to a Hollywood contract – and to near-instant stardom when he was picked to play the title role in *Captain Blood* (1935).

The next few years were Flynn's heyday. On screen, he starred dashingly in a succession of rousing costume pictures; though he may not have been an actor of wide range, he acquitted himself well enough in more demanding roles like the doomed figures of the Earl of Essex in *The Private Lives Of Elizabeth And Essex* (1939) and General Custer in *They Died With Their Boots On* (1941), displaying a hint of appealing vulnerability beneath the smooth, moustachioed surface, and much charm. Off-screen, gossip columns celebrated his alleged exploits in the boudoir and on the bottle.

Despite his impressive appearance, Flynn was not in good health – he had a heart defect and TB – and was rejected for war service on medical grounds. Ironically, he starred in sundry war movies including the notorious *Operation Burma* – banned for years in Britain and the source of innumerable jokes about the actor's winning the Burma campaign single-handed – as well as the remake of *The Dawn Patrol* (1938).

But the star had other worries. His philandering reputation took on a darker inflection when he was charged with the rape of two teenage girls aboard his yacht, although he was subsequently found not guilty. His drinking became chronic and he started to experiment with drugs. Debts mounted and his box-office status slumped. In 1952, with his long-suffering third wife, actress Patrice Wymore, he attempted a fresh start in Europe. But he was no businessman and his career took increasingly odd turns, like an appearance in the British musical *Lilacs In The Spring* (1954), in which he tried a soft-shoe shuffle and sang a tuneless version of *Lily of Laguna*.

The year before he died, he was cast as the alcoholic ex-matinee idol John Barrymore in *Too Much Too Soon*, and by double irony rose to the occasion with real command. Self-deluding though he might have been in some ways, one fancies that Flynn would have appreciated the joke.

· HARRISON FORD ·

· HARRISON FORD ·

Born **Chicago, Illinois, 13 July 1942**

Where Christopher Reeve had to assume tights and a cape to become a blockbuster super-hero, Harrison Ford did it with a battered trilby and a heavy growth of five o'clock shadow. These, together with a jumbo bullwhip, were the prime characteristics of Indiana Jones, two-fisted archaeologist (no less) hero of *Raiders Of The Lost Ark* (1981), subsequently granted titular status in *Indiana Jones And The Temple Of Doom* (1984). But then Ford was already a box-office name when he assumed the mantle of 'Indy', having struck it rich as Han Solo, space pilot extraordinary, in *Star Wars* (1977) and its sequels – though apparently he was only cast in that role after the first choice, Tom Selleck, proved to be inextricably tied up with the *Magnum P.I.* TV series.

Tall and square-jawed, with soft brown hair and not quite so soft brown eyes, Ford is good-looking, but in a – well, rather ordinary way. Perhaps it was the forthrightness of the Solo character, not to mention that of 'Indy', which caused his personality to 'gell' on the screen.

The actor was in fact 35 when *Star Wars* changed his fortunes. His first film appearance was made as early as 1966, when he played a bellboy with a single line of dialogue in *Dead Heat On A Merry-Go-Round*. He was one of the last of the contract players, briefly signed up by Columbia – other unnoticed appearances came in *A Time For Killing* (1967) and *Luv* (1968) – and in his own words, 'a baby actor getting nowhere'. Indeed, he became convinced of this to the extent of abandoning acting altogether for some time and making a living as a builder and carpenter. He returned to movies via the good offices of a friend who was casting director for *American Graffiti* (1973); his part in this may have been small, but he clicked in it, thus paving the way to Solo.

Between *Star Wars* and its sequel, *The Empire Strikes Back* (1980), Ford made several not very distinguished pictures, among them *Hanover Street* (1979), a wartime weepie which confirmed the suspicion that his charisma needed a strong script to draw it out – something *Raiders* readily achieved. Subsequently, though, he ventured into a blockbuster of more adult calibre, Ridley Scott's much praised *Blade Runner* (1982). Here, playing a Bogart-type detective in a decrepit Los Angeles of the 21st century, he achieved a quality of pathos, hard-bitten though it might be, which the action-man roles had denied him. With his hair cut raggedly short, he took on a kind of pugnacity which interestingly contrasted with a new-found suggestion of vulnerability.

Ford, now divorced, is the father of two teenage sons, and the boyfriend of Melissa Mathison, screenwriter of *E.T.* (1982); between them they can have few financial worries, although they apparently live in (by Hollywood standards) unostentatious style, having neither a screening-room nor even a swimming pool. Carpenter though he may be, it seems unlikely that he will have any concern in the foreseeable future over doing his own repairs.

· CLARK GABLE ·

· CLARK GABLE ·

Born **Cadiz, Ohio**, 1 February 1901 Died 1960

Two words sum up Clark Gable: the King. This is what they called him during the heyday of the movies in the 30s and 40s, when he was the pre-eminent male star in the firmament of Hollywood's most prestigious studio, MGM. And as Rhett Butler, the cocksure, Byronic 'visitor from Natchez' of *Gone With The Wind*, he has been enshrined as Culver City's perennial masculine archetype. 'Frankly, my dear, I don't give a damn', Rhett Butler tells Scarlett O'Hara (Vivien Leigh) in the movies' most celebrated exit line, as requited love makes way for patriotic duty. The declaration sums up Gable's essential appeal – the man who can (in all senses) take women or leave them alone.

Gable was signed up by MGM in 1931 – aged 30 – but his early life had been an uphill climb. The son of an itinerant oil-driller, he had sundry jobs as lumberjack and salesman interspersed with work in a travelling theatre troupe. But eventually he made it to Broadway, thence to Hollywood. Once success came, it came fast. Despite early doubts about his jug ears ('That guy looks like a taxi cab with both doors open' was reportedly the rude description from one Hollywood mogul), Gable became a box-office power within a couple of years. In retrospect, the seal seemed to be set on his star status when he affected the moustache which was to be the focal item in his image, complementing his rumpled, even homely,

features with a dash of the rakish and devil-may-care.

Gable was a personality actor rather than a characteriser, but his skill in inflecting his sardonic masculinity into differing spheres – action pictures, romantic melodramas, comedies – was formidable, and in 1934 he won an Oscar as the hard-boiled, soft-hearted newspaperman of *It Happened One Night*. In 1939, the year of GWTW, he married Carole Lombard and they formed Hollywood's perfect couple, even if salacious gossip had it that his great lover reputation did not extend off the set. (She was his third wife: both the others had been many years his senior.)

After war service and Lombard's tragic death in an air crash, Gable returned to MGM – it was an understandable source of rancour on his part that the huge amounts of money he had made for them were not reflected in his salary – but he was visibly ageing and some of his vehicles were indifferent. There were further, short-lived, marriages, and talk of a drinking problem. MGM dropped him in 1954, but he soldiered on. When the right movie came along, like *The Tall Men* (1955), the magnetism was still intact. And he went out in splendour as the grizzled macho idealist, opposite Marilyn Monroe, in John Huston's *The Misfits* (1961). Gable died, at 59, before the film's release – but his last performance proved clearly enough that the King had not abdicated.

· RICHARD GERE ·

· R I C H A R D   G E R E ·

Born **Syracuse, New York, 31 August 1949**

Languid is perhaps the first word one thinks of in describing the personality Richard Gere projects on the screen. Yet, almost paradoxically, the effect is linked with one of restlessness, a pantherish containment of sensuality. The face, with its slightly rosebud lips, is somewhat contradictory, too, with an openness, even ordinariness, inflected with a hint of perversity. There is a smouldering quality about the eyes, a sort of inscrutability. Gere is, in fact, very much a private man – though, according to the testimony of an ex-girlfriend, a 'very complicated' one. He is certainly inclined to shun publicity, claiming that he can't 'switch off' from a role he is playing for the convenience of visiting journalists.

In youth, Gere showed considerable musical promise: at 16, indeed, as well as playing piano and jazz guitar, he was a guest trumpet soloist with the Syracuse Symphony in the *Messiah*. He went to the University of Massachusetts – somehow, it comes as no surprise to find that he read philosophy – but dropped out to become an actor. He played in rep in Seattle, then moved to New York, having in the meantime toyed with pursuing music rather than acting. He appeared in the off-Broadway production of the musical *Grease* and later in its London production.

Eschewing TV, he had minor parts in two films, then attracted attention in *Looking For Mr Goodbar* (1977). As an oily-haired Italian stud cruising the singles bars, Gere projected a combination of allure and threat. The critic Stephen Farber went so far as to say: 'He burns up the screen and embodies the idea of sex as pure energy.' However, as the GI billeted in wartime Britain in *Yanks* (1979), Gere created a complete contrast. With cropped hair and reserved manner, he had an air of tense vulnerability fleetingly reminiscent of James Dean. Then came the memorable central role in *American Gigolo* (1979): strangely enough, this was originally destined for John Travolta, but it is difficult to imagine him in the part once one has seen Gere's portrayal. Combining narcissistic opportunism on the surface and spiritual torment beneath it, Gere exhibited a fluidity of movement which even tempts comparison with Valentino.

With *An Officer And A Gentleman* (1982, and unlike its predecessor, a huge box-office success), Gere was established as a hot property. The workings of the plot, dubious though they may be, contrived to transform an alienated working-class loner into a white-uniformed naval officer, and in the process to elevate Gere's 'outsider' to both respectability and the status of a sex object. But in the person of the nihilistic man on the run in *Breathless* (1982), the outsider was (with a moment of frontal nudity to mark the occasion) 'reborn', though in a demonstration not so much of reversion to type as of sheer versatility. Gere is very much an actor, but his star quality is second to none.

· CARY GRANT ·

· CARY GRANT ·

Real name **Archibald Leach**
Born **Bristol, England, 18 January 1904**

A journalist once despatched a telegram to Cary Grant's agent inquiring, 'How old Cary Grant?' Back came the response: 'Old Cary Grant, he just fine.' Whether or not Grant used to be coy about his age, he did not seem to make any secret of his 80th birthday. But the story is appropriate because in the past he seemed to exist almost independently of time. As he grew older, he somehow became more handsome, reaching a zenith of just-greying distinction in Hitchcock's *North By Northwest* (1959), when he was 55. Moreover, Grant was judicious enough to retire from acting when he was just turned 60 – *Walk Don't Run* (1966) was his slightly unworthy swan song – before the years could properly catch up with his appearance.

The screen roles with which Grant tends to be most closely linked – *The Philadelphia Story* (1940), *Notorious* (1946), *To Catch A Thief* (1955), *Charade* (1963) – dovetail with the notion of a man-about-town, debonair and always apt to have the last word. And this boulevardier image seemed to be complemented in his private life: five times married, four times divorced. (His second wife was the heiress Barbara Hutton, his fourth the much younger actress Dyan Cannon.)

Certainly, as a light comedian, Grant had a capacity for timing and an invisibility of technique which made him second to none. His good looks, which included an irresistible cleft chin were undeniable – as a young man he bore a more than passing resemblance to Gary Cooper, but he was less rangy and (naturally) less intrinsically American. But allied to his physical attributes and his gentleman's air, was a hint of raffishness, of caddishness even, and it was surely this undertone of contradiction which gave Grant his essential appeal.

His origins were, in fact, both colourful and humble. He ran away from a broken home to join an acrobatic troupe, then travelled to America, eking out a precarious living in such pursuits as stilt-walking sandwich-board man, before returning to England and making a modest reputation in musical comedies. This led him back to Broadway and to a Hollywood contract. Soon afterwards, Mae West – whom he acknowledged as a professional influence – chose him as her leading man in two movies, and he was on the way up.

By the late 1930s he was a sure-fire name and he remained one for three decades. He occasionally ventured into offbeat parts, as in the Cockney whimsy of *None But The Lonely Heart* (1944), but essentially he was a personality actor. As he himself once said, 'I play myself to perfection'. A kind of modernity attached to his screen presence, and he almost never essayed a costume role: *The Pride And The Passion* (1957) is one of the rare exceptions.

On retiring from acting, Grant became an executive of the Fabergé cosmetics corporation and, with characteristic insouciance, has declared that his only interest in the films he made was commercial. One begs to differ: even Fabergé could not bottle the essence of Cary Grant, but it will, thankfully, exist forever in the light of a projector.

· STEVE McQUEEN ·

· S T E V E M c Q U E E N ·

Born **Slater, Missouri, 24 March 1930** Died **7 November 1980**

Something of a conundrum attaches to Steve McQueen, who died from cancer when he was only 50. He was one of the top box-office draws of the later 60s and the 70s, and in some respects his image was akin to that of Clint Eastwood – the taciturn man of action or bemused romantic comedian. However, there was a further dimension to McQueen: like Marlon Brando and Paul Newman, he had studied at the Actors Studio (home of the 'Method') and something of the denim-clad rebel without a cause seemed to cling to him. His early life, at any rate, speaks of a degree of alienation. Having been abandoned in infancy, he subsequently spent a couple of years in a reform school, then worked at such occupations as fairground barker until he joined the Marine Corps. In his early 20s he took up acting, appearing before too long in the Broadway production of an acclaimed play about drug addiction, *A Hatful Of Rain*.

His movie career began in such deathless B-feature efforts as *The Blob* (1958), but in 1960 a role in the Western, *The Magnificent Seven*, turned him into someone to reckon with. Three years later came another hugely popular film, the POW adventure *The Great Escape* (1963). McQueen's role in this movie crystallised his on-screen personality as a combination of taciturn outsider and daredevil. It was also widely advertised that he insisted on performing his own stunts for the motor-bike chase sequence. This reflects the actor's off-screen enthusiasm for car and motorbike racing – and the internal combustion engine does indeed seem central to McQueen's acting career. *Bullitt* (1968) is chiefly renowned for its car chase and the title of *Le Mans* (1971) speaks for itself.

His aura of self-sufficient manliness chimed in with his dislike of publicity about his private life (he was married for four years to the actress Ali McGraw). But if this constituted one part of the McQueen persona, it was not the whole story. Pictures like *Love With The Proper Stranger* (1964), the neglected *Baby, The Rain Must Fall* (1964), and the glossy ambiguous, *The Thomas Crown Affair* (1968), testified to the actor's readiness to open up a vein of bitterness and romantic vulnerability, along with a wry streak of humour.

Bullet-headed and slightly ungainly, McQueen was distinctive rather than conventionally handsome, though his eyes were as piercingly blue as Newman's and his smile angelic. He was apt to gravitate – though it may have been out of a sense for the profit motive – to portentous blockbusters like *Papillon* (1973), but there is no doubt that McQueen took acting seriously – seriously enough, indeed, to venture into a film version, which he produced himself, of no less than Ibsen's *An Enemy Of The People* (1977). He also seemingly wished to follow Newman and Redford into turning director. Sadly, though, fate denied him the chance. In one of his last movies, *Tom Horn* (1979), he was cast as a man for whom time has run out: the haggard dignity of his performance becomes in retrospect profoundly touching.

· PAUL NEWMAN ·

· PAUL NEWMAN ·

Born **Cleveland, Ohio, 26 January 1925**

Although he was actually born a few years before James Dean, Paul Newman was in several respects Dean's natural successor – and not simply because the two men were friends or because the film which established Newman's reputation, *Somebody Up There Likes Me* (1956), a biopic about the boxer Rocky Graziano, had originally been earmarked for Dean. Newman inherited Dean's aura of denim-clad non-conformity and his air of defensive romanticism. But while as a young man Newman had a slightness which, like Dean's, carried an implication of vulnerability, he was both of more impressive physical build and more conventionally handsome. In a way, Newman's rounded, finely proportioned features are those of the middle-class ideal; indeed, contrary to the image projected by some of his early screen roles, he had come from a conventional white-collar background.

His father ran a successful sporting goods store and Newman saw wartime service in the Navy Air Corps before embarking on an economics course at university. It was there that he was bitten by the acting bug, and he went on to Yale Drama School and studied at the Actors' Studio. His early success on Broadway as the footloose hero of *Picnic* led to film offers, though his first movie – an absurd biblical spectacular, *The Silver Chalice* (1955) – proved something of a false start.

With the Graziano film, however, Newman was hailed as a movie star in the new mould. In quick succession, several other films established both his versatility and the strength of his claim to be a definitively modern leading man. There was the inarticulately intense Billy the Kid of *The Left Handed Gun* (1958); the smoulderingly sensual loner of *The Long Hot Summer* (1958); above all, the outwardly exquisite, inwardly ravaged protagonist of *Cat On A Hot Tin Roof* (1958). The latter brought his first Oscar nomination – though despite no fewer than four subsequent nominations (*The Hustler*, 1961, *Hud*, 1963, *Cool Hand Luke*, 1967, *The Verdict*, 1982) he has yet to carry off the award.

While Newman branched out into a wide gamut of material, showing an increasing penchant for comedy, his star power remained undimmed. He has grown bulkier with the advancing years, but to say that he has aged gracefully would be an understatement: at 60, he could pass easily for 10 years less. The blueness of his eyes is perhaps his most striking feature – they are surely bluer than the Mediterranean – and the quality of their gaze seems to betoken clearsightedness in the management of his affairs.

He is acting less nowadays, but has directed several films, mostly starring Joanne Woodward, his wife since 1958. Newman is a car racing devotee in his leisure time, but eschews the glare of publicity. His urge for privacy can, indeed, sometimes be fierce. On a recent visit to a London theatre, the story goes, a fan approached and nervously inquired if he really was Paul Newman. 'I should hope not,' the star snapped back. 'I hear he's a real shit.'

· GREGORY PECK ·

· GREGORY PECK ·

Born **La Jolla, California, 5 April 1916**

Tall, dark and handsome is the phrase that springs unbidden to mind when attempting to describe Gregory Peck. When he began to appear in films in the mid-1940s, he could fairly have been called classically good-looking; the slightly sharp, even Slavic cast of his features lends distinctiveness to his appearance, indeed enhancing his appeal.

As a young man he was of comparatively slight build, and this, allied with his height, gave him a seeming air of vulnerability which contrasted with the determination signalled by his dark, deep-set eyes. In growing older, he has become bulkier, yet at the same time his features seem to have become more aquiline, more Lincolnesque: it was surely inevitable that he should one day play Abraham Lincoln, as he did in a TV production of 1981.

Peck was the son of modestly impoverished parents, but went to the prestigious University of California at Berkeley, where he began to harbour literary ambitions. Though he had never acted before, he appeared in several student productions, and opted to make acting his career. This was not accomplished without initial hardship, but within a few years he was attracting sufficient attention on Broadway to arouse the interest of Hollywood. He was, in fact, early on offered an MGM contract, but turned it down on the grounds of seeing himself primarily as a stage actor; indeed, several years later, after he became a film star, he was instrumental in setting up a summer playhouse in his birthplace of La Jolla so as to keep his links with live theatre.

The actor's first movie was *Days Of Glory* (1944), which was cast with 'unknowns' and allowed him to make his debut in a leading role. Next came the demanding part of the missionary priest in the film which really established him, *The Keys Of The Kingdom* (1944): it brought him an Oscar nomination, though it was not until 1963 that *To Kill A Mockingbird* allowed him to carry off the coveted award. He has said that he derives most pleasure from comedy roles and that the highest professional compliment he has received was to be commended by veteran comic George Burns for the quality of his reaction in *Designing Woman* (1957) to having a plate of pasta tipped into his lap by an indignant lady-friend. But he has often been prepared to play against easy sympathy: as the stress-torn commander in *Twelve O'Clock High* (1949), for instance, or as a steely avenger in *The Bravados* (1958).

In private life, Peck has lived expensively but decorously – he has been married twice, but neither wife was from show business – and has been associated with a variety of liberal and charitable causes. And he has certainly aged gracefully. As he said himself about *The Omen* (1976), which marked something of a comeback after several years away from acting, there aren't too many actors around to be cast as the United States ambassador to the Court of St James.

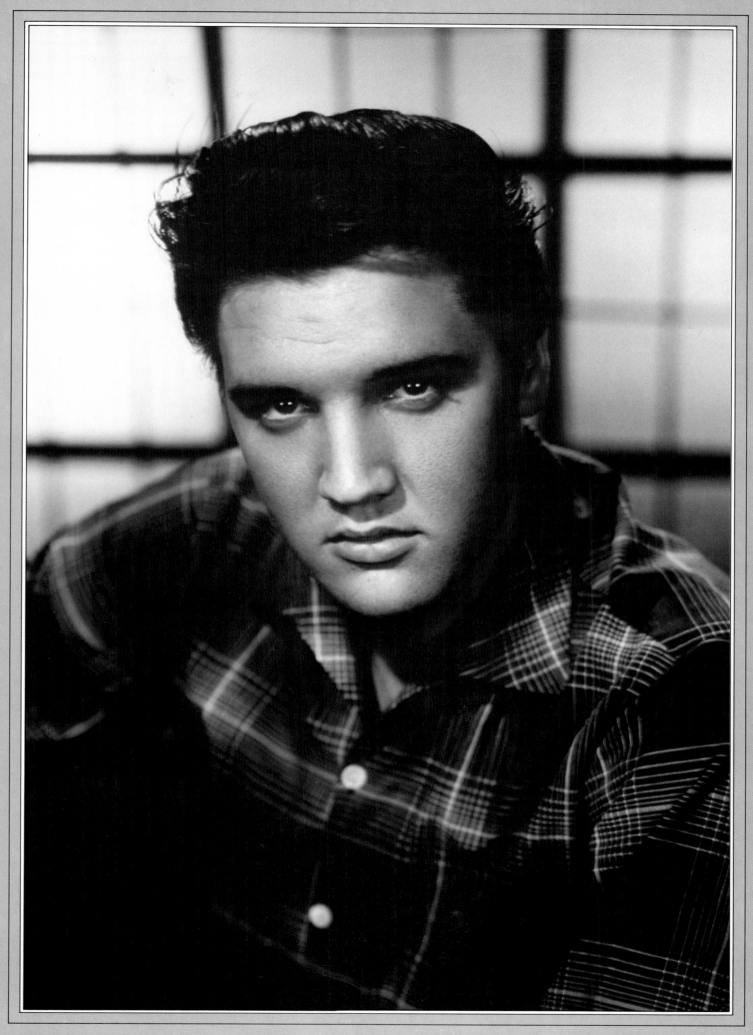

· ELVIS PRESLEY ·

· E L V I S   P R E S L E Y ·

Born **Tuppelo, Missouri, 8 January 1935** Died **16 August 1977**

'Elvis the Pelvis' they called him when he burst on to the pop music scene in 1956 with his record of 'Heartbreak Hotel'. The sobriquet was appropriately unambiguous: when Elvis performed on TV in the early days, camera operators were instructed to show him only from the waist up.

It may seem difficult, three decades on, in the light of the punk craze or even of the Rolling Stones, to appreciate what the fuss was all about – though not, surely, still to enjoy the unaffected energy of the recordings themselves. Elvis provided a fresh focus for the phenomenon of rock 'n' roll, replacing the genial frenzy of the kiss-curled Bill Haley (*Rock Around The Clock*) with the brooding, leather-clad presence of a Marlon Brando.

Yet there was a directness – even a kind of innocence – about Presley. A somewhat later pop performer, Mick Jagger, had the same sensual mouth and galvanic intensity; but where Jagger on stage projected a bisexual ambiguity, Presley – with his black leather and oiled shock of hair – was completely direct. (And perhaps by utilising elements of what had previously been considered black music, his performances also administered a shock of a different kind.)

Elvis was 20 when he became an overnight sensation. The survivor of identical twins, he had grown up from the age of 13 in the hillbilly heartland of Memphis, Tennessee, and had worked as a truck driver while playing with local bands. Subsequently, as one golden disc gave way to another – among

them the sublimely surreal 'Blue Suede Shoes' – Presley accomplished an inevitable transition to the movies, though his debut, curiously, was as a bad-hat in the Western, *Love Me Tender* (1956). To an extent, *Jailhouse Rock* (1957) and *King Creole* (1958), the latter derived from a Harold Robbins novel, provided an apt showcase for Presley's moody energy.

But in 1958, the singer received his army call-up, and his manager, the indefatigable 'Colonel' Tom Parker, decreed that he should not seek to waive the obligation. This paved the way to a 'new' Elvis, a cleaned-up exponent of family entertainment. The records he later made retained something of the old verve, though inevitably their effect was shading into conventionality. However, Presley's career was heavily committed during the 1960s to films, and the pictures he prolifically turned out during the decade mark a regression into the anodyne and inane. Titles like *Girls! Girls! Girls!* (1962) and *Easy Come, Easy Go* (1966) should perhaps be left to speak for themselves.

In 1969 Presley had a resounding success in concert in Las Vegas and subsequent concert tours were sell-outs: the magnetism was still there, even if the showbiz trappings of his stage act were pushing toward parody. But he was increasingly overweight, living reclusively on quantities of junk food and (it transpired) dependent on drugs. By the time he died of a heart attack at 42, the once undisputed monarch of rock 'n' roll had become its unwitting court jester.

·ROBERT REDFORD·

· ROBERT REDFORD ·

Born **Santa Monica, California, 18 August 1937**

There was a kind of appropriateness about Robert Redford's being teamed with Paul Newman in the hugely successful *Butch Cassidy And The Sundance Kid* in 1969. Not that Newman's career was declining – witness *The Sting*, in which he and Redford renewed their partnership four years later – but nonetheless the mantle was in a sense being passed on from one husky blond star to a younger substitute. As Newman edged toward character roles, Redford became the essential romantic star of the early 70s.

It is somewhat surprising to realise that Redford had played in only six films before incarnating the Sundance Kid, epitome of the acceptable face of dropping out. But supporting roles in *Inside Daisy Clover* and *The Chase*, both in 1966, offered clear intimations of his star quality. In both films, he was cast as a self-destructive, impulsive figure; and what lends him his charisma is surely a dichotomy between the placidity and assurance which attach to his classically handsome appearance, and the vein of insecurity or neurosis which his more interesting roles have mined.

The son of an accountant, Redford conformed to traditional pattern to the extent of winning a baseball scholarship to university, and then, veering toward a more recent stereotype, dropped out of college to travel around Europe with the aim of becoming a painter. Back in the US, he took up drama, making his Broadway debut in 1959 and achieving stardom in the Neil Simon comedy *Barefoot In The Park* in

1963. The subsequent movie version (1967) gave him Hollywood top billing opposite Jane Fonda; then came *Butch Cassidy* and his position was secured. That film seemed to establish him as the thinking person's pin-up, and a sort of seriousness clings to Redford's public image. As well as supporting various liberal causes, he is active on behalf of conservation and runs film-making workshops at his Utah ranch. Yet Redford's sheer physical glamour may have circumscribed him as an actor. In *The Way We Were* (1973), for instance, with Barbra Streisand, Redford carries with him an inbuilt poise which risks making the character's vacillation in love and politics difficult to credit.

Still, his being cast in the title role of *The Great Gatsby* (1974) was surely as axiomatic as Clark Gable's selection to play Rhett Butler. Doubts may be in order about the adaptation of Scott Fitzgerald's novel, but Redford unquestionably embodied its ambiguous, white-suited hero to perfection – a reminder that romanticism can be all the more potent for seeming somehow superficial.

When Redford turned director, it was with a low-key domestic drama, *Ordinary People* (1980), in which he did not himself appear. And when he returned to acting after a hiatus with *The Natural* (1984), it was in the guise of a one-time wonder boy who is granted a second chance in life . . . Redford, one feels, will have no shortage of future chances, but he prefers to keep his distance from his own aura.

· CHRISTOPHER REEVE ·

·CHRISTOPHER REEVE·

Born New York City, 25 September 1952

As far as his screen career goes, Christopher Reeve got off to a literally flying start by being cast in the title role of the blockbuster *Superman* (1978). His early background, though, was closer in spirit to the Clark Kent side of the character than to the beefcake one. His father was an academic, his mother a journalist, and there was no acting blood in the family at all.

However, the youthful Reeve had an abiding fascination with the theatre, which he put into practice by signing up at the age of 15 with a repertory company, the Williamstown Players. He went to Cornell University, but continued to fit studies around a burgeoning career as an actor. His master's thesis was on European theatre, and he 'researched' it by coming to England, visiting various rep companies and getting a temporary job at the Old Vic.

Launched into full-time acting, Reeve played in TV, including a spell in a daytime soap opera, and appeared on Broadway in the play *A Matter of Gravity* opposite no less than Katherine Hepburn, an experience he values highly. And then he won an audition for the lead in *Superman*, though he has said that having been chosen, the (literal) build-up to the filming was arduous – it required him to put on more than 30 lb of muscle, apparently achieved via a high-protein diet as well as intensive working-out in the gym. Reeve looked the part to perfection. He stands over six foot, with blue eyes and somewhat soft, even boyish, features qualified by distinctively high cheekbones. In the non-Superman parts of *Superman*,

Reeve showed an engaging, James Stewart-style diffidence, which lent itself well to the comic passages that were expanded in the (actually livelier) sequels.

Translated into super-stardom by *Superman*, Reeve did not allow himself to be restricted to blockbusters. His next film was the intimate *Somewhere In Time* (1980), in which he effectively impersonated a playwright, and in *Deathtrap* (1982), from Ira Levin's hit play, he was a playwright again, though this time of a dubious sort. Moreover, in the latter movie he was not merely a largely unsympathetic character, but risked going against the box-office grain to the extent of playing a homosexual and, at one point, even exchanging a kiss with the usually equally macho Michael Caine.

But it was as the opportunistic Basil Ransom in *The Bostonians* (1984) that Reeve achieved his most challenging and probably most authoritative role. In this Henry James adaptation, his hair is slicked and black, the 1880s wardrobe he sports lends him a rakish quality that brings out both the dominance of his physique and a certain undertone of pathos, and his immense frame and maturing and striking good looks are a powerful component of the film itself.

Reeve's English-born girlfriend, with whom he has lived in unobtrusively affluent style for several years and by whom he has two children, describes him as 'very un-jetsetty'. Despite having waved goodbye to Superman, however, he seems liable to be flying high for quite a while.

· BURT REYNOLDS ·

· BURT REYNOLDS ·

Born **Waycross, Georgia, 11 February 1936**

There is something about Burt Reynolds of the card – the joker in the pack. It is not just that in recent years he has carved a niche for himself in boisterous 'redneck' comedies; there is an aura about the man himself – the moustache he often adopts, the expanse of flashing teeth revealed in a wide grin – which seems not quite real, an amiable parody of what one hesitates to call cocksureness. His macho appearance has something very much in common with that of Clark Gable, but with Reynolds there is a hovering element of both self-consciousness and self-mockery.

Born in Georgia and raised in Florida, Reynolds grew up in the 'sun belt' South, where his redneck movies like *Smokey And The Bandit* (1977) have earned their biggest profits. His father was none other than chief of police, and Reynolds had a difficult childhood, though he later became a high school football star and won a football scholarship to university. Injuries caused him to take up drama instead, and he moved to New York, then on to Hollywood.

His film debut came as early as 1962 with a small part in the independent feature *Angel Baby*, but his career did not exactly prosper and he sometimes had to turn stuntman to make a living. In the mid-1960s he was married for three years to the irrepressible Judy Carne, of TV *Laugh-In* fame, but the marriage foundered, perhaps partly because wife was dramatically out-earning the husband. Reynolds, however, gradually gained more prominence, in TV series like *Dan August* and *Hawk* (in the latter, playing an Indian detective – Reynolds' paternal grandmother was a Cherokee Indian) and in some routine, action-oriented movies.

Then came an engagement as guest host of the *Tonight Show*, in which Reynolds – who was now escort to the singer Dinah Shore, 19 years his senior – chose as chief guest his ex-wife Judy Carne, with whom he proceeded to conduct a quite intimate conversation. This display of bravado led to his being cast in *Deliverance* (1972), his first 'serious' film. But it seems typical of Reynolds' cheerful capacity to take a chance that the film's release virtually coincided with his being featured as a nude centrefold (actually quite modest) in *Cosmopolitan* magazine.

Soon, anyway, Reynolds was a bankable star, generally in extrovert roles but occasionally tackling something deeper. Like his friend Clint Eastwood, he turned to direction, with *Gator* (1976), an odd comedy, *The End* (1978), and the thriller *Sharky's Machine* (1982). The last he dubbed 'Dirty Harry goes to Atlanta', joking that if Eastwood could venture into his domain of redneck farce, he was entitled to reciprocate. Leaving aside his unwise penchant for appearing in musicals (*At Long Last Love*, 1975; *The Best Little Whorehouse In Texas*, 1982), there seems no reason why the joker should not be profitably wild for some time to come.

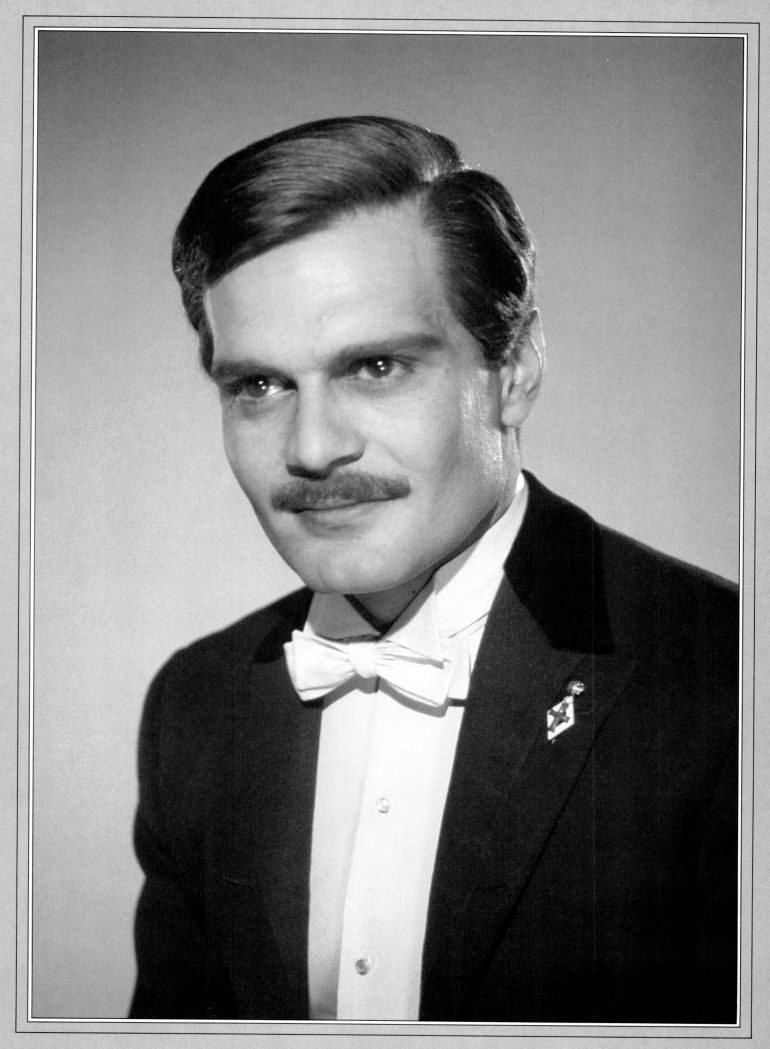

· OMAR SHARIF ·

· O M A R   S H A R I F ·

Real Name **Michael Shalhoub**
Born **Alexandria, Egypt, 10 April 1932**

Ever since Valentino the hunt has been on for Latin lovers to take his place. But if many would-be successors have been called by the studios, few have been chosen by the public. Who now, for instance, remembers such contenders as Ricardo Montalban? In the early 1960s, however, there came along – never mind that he was Egyptian rather than Latin – an unmistakable contender for the title ... Omar Sharif, who burst upon the consciousness of western moviegoers as a tribal chieftain in *Lawrence of Arabia* (1962).

Sharif had been a screen star in his native land for several years before David Lean cast him in *Lawrence*. The son of a wealthy importer, he had received a western-style education and had briefly worked as a salesman in his father's firm before becoming an actor. He appeared in some two dozen Egyptian films, and his popularity as an Arab matinee idol was enhanced when he married Egypt's leading female star Fatem Hamama (the marriage ended in divorce). Once *Lawrence* was released, garnering him an Oscar nomination, his future in the international cinema was assured. Sharif in his prime certainly had a commanding physical presence – tall, moustachioed and debonair, with shining black hair, flashing eyes, and a swarthy sense of 'otherness.'

Not surprisingly, he tended to be cast in costume roles calling for swagger and braggadoccio, appearing as Marco Polo and even Genghis Khan in assorted epics before playing his most famous part, again for Lean, the title character in *Dr Zhivago* (1965). Somewhat miscast and certainly not a good enough actor for Pasternak's hero, the role nonetheless brought out a soulful, somehow rather passive quality in Sharif, a kind of romantic languor that was not ineffective. A little later, playing opposite Barbra Streisand in the musical *Funny Girl* (1968) – where Sharif cautiously ventured into song – he brought something of the same quality to a role of seemingly different stamp, that of a high-living gambler. At any rate, he must have felt at home handling cards: he is a bridge player of international class and has been the leader of a successful international team. Moreover, he has tended to live a playboy-like, jetsetting social life and, unlike the character in *Funny Girl*, has held on to his money.

As time went by, however, Omar's acting opportunities showed some decline, even leaving aside his being called on to impersonate Che Guevara in the miscalculated *Che!* (1969). In *Juggernaut* (1974), he revealed a sharper sense of irony, and perhaps a more genuine capacity for feeling, than had earlier been the case; on the whole, though, he was being relegated to cameo parts, like the villain in *Ashanti* (1979).

In a way, advancing years have brought out a stolidity in Sharif and (as far as his screen personality goes) a certain lack of spontaneity. But then, perhaps Latin lovers are apt to fade away rather than grow old.

· R U D O L P H   V A L E N T I N O ·

· RUDOLPH VALENTINO ·

Real name **Rudolfo Guglielmi**
Born **Castellaneta, Italy, 6 May 1895** Died **23 August 1926**

'Just a good-looking, lucky guy, who copped a sensational role and a good cameraman': this was how Rex Ingram, director of *The Four Horsemen Of The Apocalypse* (1921), later described the actor whom it made a star, Rudolph Valentino. Ingram was hardly a dispassionate observer – he evidently felt that the cult which surrounded Valentino detracted from recognition of his own efforts – and his remark is hardly an adequate explanation of the Valentino phenomenon.

However, it is true as far as it goes. Valentino was not only good looking – in an 'un-American' way which exercised an extra appeal at the dawn of the roaring twenties – he was also undeniably lucky in finding in *Horsemen* a vehicle tailored so expertly, and not just in the immortal tango sequence, to reveal his novelty for American audiences.

Sixty years on, it is probably impossible to pin down Valentino's appeal, to separate the reality from the semi-caricatural stereotype of the patent leather-haired 'Latin lover' – an image which, at the time, Valentino himself strongly resented. Alexander Walker has written of Valentino's having 'an elegance, an enormous delicacy in his movements . . . unlike those of other American actors of the time'. And it is surely of the utmost significance that Valentino had been a professional dancer before becoming an actor.

He had arrived in the US from Italy at the age of 18 and found the going tough. Subsequently he became a 'taxi dancer' – a kind of ballroom gigolo – before moving up the scale to partner the exhibition dancer, Bonnie Glass. But he was still dogged by ill luck and after trouble with the law, 'escaped' to California by travelling in the cast of a touring musical. Film parts followed and in 1920 he married actress Jean Acker: it is one more aspect of the Valentino mystery that the brief marriage was evidently never consummated.

The breakthrough of *Horsemen* was consolidated by his next and most famous (if actually much cruder) film *The Sheikh* (1921). Here he is the exotic seducer par excellence, the Arab chief who carries off an English girl into the desert. Bets are hedged, however, to the extent that seduction never actually ensues and the 'Arab' is finally revealed as none other than a British nobleman with marriage in mind. Valentino became immensely rich, dabbled in spiritualism, published a volume of verse (the dedication to 'GS' referred not, as some supposed, to Gloria Swanson but to George Sand), was charged with bigamy and attacked in the press as a 'pansy'. He had sought out a wider variety of roles, but was driven back in *Son Of The Sheikh* (1926) to the exotic, erotic, stereotype his (largely female) public demanded. It was to be his last film.

His death at 31 from a perforated ulcer provoked riots and suicides. How he might have adapted to sound movies and the onset of middle age we shall never know, but as a phenomenon and a legend he remains unique.